FOR YOUR BIRTHDAY

Edited by Jill Wolf

ISBN 0-89954-446-0

CONTENTS

I wish you all the joy that you can wish.

—_William Shakespeare_

Most of us can remember a time when a birthday . . . brightened the world as if a second sun had risen.

—_Robert Lynd_

The Gift of Living   23

Thank God for life, with all its endless store
Of great experiences . . .

—Thomas Durley Landels

The Best Is Yet to Be   45

Grow old along with me!
The best is yet to be . . .

—Robert Browning

 BIRTHDAY WISHES

For a Birthday

So much that I would give you hovers out
Of reach of my poor giving—song within
Your heart forever, faith to end all doubt,
And laughter, warm and gold,
    when you begin
To grow too serious, and, always near,
The good companionship of trees
    and birds;
And always, for your beauty-loving ear,
Music for when you have need of it
    and words
That pleasure you and rest you,
    softly spoken;
Unnumbered good days, peace of
    a starry night,
And love from dawn to dawn that's
    an unbroken
Deep certainty in you . . . . I have no right
To dream of it—but never doubt I should
Give you such birthday presents, if I could.

—*Elaine V. Emans*

Believing, hear what you deserve to hear;
Your birthday as my own to me is dear.
Blest and distinguish'd days!
     which we should prize;
The first, the kindest bounty of the skies.
But yours gives most; for mine
     did only lend
Me to the world; yours gave to me
     a friend.

—Martial

May your days be good and long upon
the earth.

—American Indian Saying

God grant you many and happy years . . .

—Oliver Wendell Holmes

God Be with You

May His Counsels Sweet uphold you,
And His Loving Arms enfold you,
As you journey on your way.

May His Sheltering Wings protect you,
And His Light Divine direct you,
Turning darkness into day.

May His Potent Peace surround you,
And His Presence linger with you,
As your inner, golden ray.

—Author Unknown

A Birthday Wish

I do not wish you joy
    without a sorrow,
Nor endless day without
    the healing dark,
Nor brilliant sun without
    the restful shadow,
Nor tides that never turn
    against your bark.

I wish you love, and strength,
    and faith, and wisdom,
Goods, gold enough to help
    some needy one.
I wish you songs, but also
    blessed silence,
And God's sweet peace
    when every day is done.

—Dorothy Nell McDonald

God Bless You

I seek in prayerful words, dear friend,
My heart's true wish to send you,
That you may know that, far or near,
My loving thoughts attend you.

I cannot find a truer word,
Nor better to address you;
Nor song, nor poem have I heard
Is sweeter than God bless you!

God bless you! So I've wished you all
Of brightness life possesses;
For can there any joy at all
Be yours unless God blesses?

God bless you! So I breathe a charm
Lest grief's dark night oppress you,
For how can sorrow bring you harm
If 'tis God's way to bless you?

And so, "through all thy days
May shadows touch thee never—"
But this alone—God bless thee—
Then art thou safe forever.

—*Author Unknown*

Written on the Road

Out in the sunshine fair and free,
Flecked by the blossoming, re-born tree,
Bathed in the pure, pale light of Spring,
While men look up, and the
　　glad birds sing,—
There, dear friend, let thy reck'ning be,
So let thy birthdays come to thee!

Firm as the tall, brave trunks around;
Full of life as the flower-full ground;
Free as the boughs that sweep the blue;
Bright as the violet's sudden hue;—
So let thy life-long reck'ning be,
So let thy birthdays come to thee!

It was cool and gray in the twilight morn—
A prophecy sweetest—when thou
　　wast born;
And if daylight gathered a cloud or two
That floated beside thee when life was new,
Thy noon will be sunny and clear, I know,
And holy and peaceful thine evening glow:
For good and true shall thy reck'ning be
Till all thy birthdays are come to thee.

—Mary Mapes Dodge

May you live all the days of your life.

—Jonathan Swift

. . . may you live for a thousand years, and
I be there to count them.

—Robert Smith Surtees

I wish you all the joy that you can wish.

—William Shakespeare

There is nothing more properly the
language of the heart than the wish.

—Robert South

Four bright candles
And one to grow on,
Five bright candles
All to blow on.

I make my mouth
Round like an O.
I wait and think,
Then wish—and blow!

—*Miriam Clark Potter*

It seems to me we can never give up
longing and wishing while we are
thoroughly alive. There are certain
things we feel to be beautiful and
good, and we must hunger after them.

—*George Eliot*

 A PERFECT DAY

Somebody's birthday every day,
Over this land so wide and far.
So let us be generous, kind and gay
For Somebody's sake, wherever we are.

—Abbie Farwell Brown

Did you ever think how queer
That, every day all through the year,
Someone has a frosted cake,
And candles for a birthday's sake?

—Rachel Field

The Birthday of the Lord

The Baby Christ, when He was born,
Was cradled in a manger—
Still He was King of all the world—
Was ever story stranger?

The shepherds came from far and wide,
And, wondering, bent above Him;
His will it was that hearts of men
Should know Him and should love Him.

The cattle breathed their breath on Him;
The little lambs pressed near Him;
His will it was that man nor beast
Should stand apart nor fear Him.

Then let your hearts be filled with joy
While Christmas bells are ringing,
And keep the birthday of the Lord
With merriment and singing.

—*Mary Jane Carr*

Most of us can remember a time when a birthday—especially if it was one's own—brightened the world as if a second sun had risen.

—Robert Lynd

It is lovely, when I forget all birthdays, including my own, to find that somebody remembers me.

—Ellen Glasgow

Her birthdays were always important to her; for being a born lover of life, she would always keep the day of her entrance into it as a very great festival indeed . . .

—Elizabeth Goudge

My birthday was a good one, being at home again, and the day was properly diversified with flowers and a call or two, a letter or two, etc.—just what a birthday ought to be.

—George E. Woodberry

Oh! to have a birthday—
Candles burning bright,
Eyes so blue and sparkling,
Happy heart so light!

—Lois Lenski

A birthday:—and now a day that rose
With much of hope, with meaning rife—
A thoughtful day from dawn to close:
The middle day of human life.

—Jean Ingelow

For Memory has painted this perfect day
With colors that never fade,
And we find at the end of a perfect day
The soul of a friend we've made.

—Carrie Jacobs Bond

A Birthday

My heart is like a singing bird
Whose nest is in a watered shoot;
My heart is like an appletree
Whose boughs are bent
   with thickset fruit;
My heart is like a rainbow shell
That paddles in a halcyon sea;
My heart is gladder than all these
Because my love is come to me.

Raise me a dais of silk and down;
Hang it with vair and purple dyes;
Carve it in doves, and pomegranates,
And peacocks with a hundred eyes;
Work it in gold and silver grapes,
In leaves, and silver fleurs-de-lys;
Because the birthday of my life
Is come, my love is come to me.

—*Christina Rossetti*

The Birthday Child

Everything's been different
All the day long,
Lovely things have happened,
Nothing has gone wrong.

Nobody has scolded me,
Everyone has smiled.
Isn't it delicious
To be a birthday child?

—*Rose Fyleman*

Birthday Cake

Christmas cakes
are anybody's cakes—
anybody's offered some
and anybody takes;
but a Birthday Cake
is your very own cake;
it's blue and silver,
pink and white,
wears little candles
all alight,
(each one for
each single year
that *you* have been
living here!)
it sparkles bright
with sugar-ice—
Oh! Birthday Cake
is VERY nice!

—*Ivy O. Eastwick*

Birthday Cake

If little mice have birthdays
(and I suppose they do)
And have a family party
(and guests invited too)
And have a cake with candles
(it would be rather small)
I bet a birthday CHEESE cake
would please them most of all.

—*Aileen Fisher*

🎁 THE GIFT OF LIVING 🎁

Do you count your birthdays thankfully?

—Horace

Reflect upon your present blessings, of
which every man has many . . .

—Charles Dickens

Thou that hast given so much to me,
Give one thing more—a grateful heart;
Not thankful when it pleaseth me,
As if Thy blessings had spare days;
But such a heart, whose pulse may be
   Thy praise.

—George Herbert

Prayer

Oh, Lord, I thank You for the privilege and gift of living in a world filled with beauty and excitement and variety.

I thank You for the gift of loving and being loved, for the friendliness and understanding and beauty of the animals on the farm and in the forest and marshes, for the green of the trees, the sound of a waterfall, the darting beauty of the trout in the brook.

I thank You for the delights of music and children, of other men's thoughts and conversation and their books to read by the fireside or in bed with the rain falling on the roof or the snow blowing past outside the window.

—*Louis Bromfield*

God's gifts put man's best dreams to shame.

—*Elizabeth Barrett Browning*

What brings joy to the heart is not so much
the friend's gift as the friend's love.

—*Aelred of Rievaulx*

Gratitude

Gratitude consists in a watchful, minute
attention to the particulars of our state,
and to the multitude of God's gifts, taken
one by one. It fills us with a conscious-
ness that God loves and cares for us, even
to the least event and smallest need of life.
It is a blessed thought that from our childhood God has been laying His fatherly
hands upon us, and always in benediction,
and that even the strokes of His hands are
blessings, and among the chiefest we have
ever received.

—*Henry Edward Manning*

At Eighty-Three

Thank God for life, with all
    its endless store
Of great experiences, of hill and dale,
Of cloud and sunshine, tempest,
    snow and hail.
Thank God for straining sinews,
    panting breast,
No less for weary slumber, peaceful rest;
Thank God for home and parents,
    children, friends,
For sweet companionship that
    never ends;
Thank God for all the splendor
    of the earth,
For nature teeming with prolific birth;
Thank God for sea and sky,
    for changing hours,
For trees and singing birds
    and fragrant flowers.
And so in looking back at eighty-three
My final word to you, my friends, shall be:
Thank God for life; and when
    the gift's withdrawn,
Thank God for twilight bell,
    and coming dawn.

—Thomas Durley Landels

Be glad of life because it gives you the
chance to love and to work and to play
and to look up at the stars . . .

—Henry van Dyke

The south wind is driving
His splendid cloud-horses
Through vast fields of blue.
The bare woods are singing,
The brooks in their courses
Are bubbling and springing,
And dancing and leaping,
The violets peeping,
I'm glad to be living:
Aren't you?

—Gamaliel Bradford

I make the most of all that comes,
And the least of all that goes.

—Sara Teasdale

For everything you have missed, you have
gained something else.

—Ralph Waldo Emerson

One cannot collect all the beautiful shells
on the beach; one can collect only a few,
and they are more beautiful if they are few.

—Anne Morrow Lindbergh

This day is all that is good and fair. It is
too dear, with its hopes and invitations, to
waste a moment on the yesterdays.

—Ralph Waldo Emerson

Happiness is a butterfly which, when pursued, is always just beyond your grasp, but which, if you will sit down quietly, may alight upon you.

—Nathaniel Hawthorne

Happiness is not having what you want, but wanting what you have.

—Hyman Schachtel

Happiness is not a station you arrive at, but a manner of traveling.

—Margaret Lee Runbeck

Life is not always what one wants it to be,
but to make the best of it as it is, is the
only way of being happy.

—*Jennie Jerome Churchill*

Life is a series of surprises, and would not
be worth taking or keeping if it were not.

—*Ralph Waldo Emerson*

Count Your Garden

Count your garden by the flowers,
Never by the leaves that fall;
Count your days by golden hours;
Don't remember clouds at all.

Count the nights by stars, not shadows;
Count your life by smiles, not tears;
And with joy on every birthday,
Count your age by friends, not years.

—*Author Unknown*

The Salutation of the Dawn

Listen to the Exhortation of the Dawn!
Look to this Day!
For it is Life, the very Life of Life.
In its brief course lie all the
Verities and Realities of your Existence:
The Bliss of Growth,
The Glory of Action,
The Splendor of Beauty,
For Yesterday is but a Dream,
And Tomorrow is only a Vision:
But Today well-lived makes
Every Yesterday a Dream of Happiness,
And every Tomorrow a Vision of Hope.
Look well therefore to this Day!
Such is the Salutation of the Dawn!

—based on the Sanskrit

Three Days

Yesterday . . .
Like mintage spent, is past recall;
Its echo dimmed beyond time's wall.

Tomorrow . . .
It never promised earthly man,
Nor does it often fit a plan.

Today . . .
Is gold that covers hill and dell,
And rich are they who use it well.

—*Pearl Phillips*

Nothing is more highly to be prized than
the value of each day.

—*Johann Wolfgang von Goethe*

Write it on your heart that every day is the
best day in the year.

—*Ralph Waldo Emerson*

New Year's Day is every man's birthday.

—*Charles Lamb*

Every day is a fresh beginning,
Every morn is the world made new.

—*Susan Coolidge*

Be not afraid of life. Believe that life *is* worth living, and your belief will help create the fact.

—*William James*

I would be always in the thick of life,
Threading its mazes, sharing its strife,
Yet—somehow singing!

—*Roselle Mercier Montgomery*

The time God allots to each one of us is like a precious tissue which we embroider as best we know how.

—*Anatole France*

Our life is a gift from God. What we do with that life is our gift to God.

—*Author Unknown*

The great use of life is to spend it for something that outlasts it.

—*William James*

We are here to add what we can to, not to get what we can from, life.

—*Sir William Osler*

There is no duty we underrate so
much as the duty of being happy.

—Robert Louis Stevenson

Do your best to turn your life into a
festival.

—Johann Wolfgang von Goethe

The days that make us happy make
us wise.

—John Masefield

Serene will be our days and bright,
And happy will our nature be,
When love is an unerring light,
And joy its own security.

—*William Wordsworth*

The time you enjoy wasting is not wasted time.

—*Bertrand Russell*

One ought, every day at least, to hear a little song, read a good poem, see a fine picture . . .

—*Johann Wolfgang von Goethe*

With a few flowers in my garden, half a dozen pictures and some books, I live without envy.

—*Lope de Vega*

I know well that happiness is in little
things . . .

—John Ruskin

The happiness of life is made up of minute
fractions . . . a kiss or smile, a kind look, a
heartfelt compliment . . .

—Samuel Taylor Coleridge

Life's sweetest joys are hidden
In unsubstantial things;
An April rain, a fragrance,
A vision of blue wings . . .

—May Riley Smith

Daily Joys

There is only one thing about which I
shall have no regrets when my life ends. I
have savored to the full all the small daily
joys. The bright sunshine on the breakfast
table; the smell of the air at dusk; the
sound of the clock ticking; the light rains
that start gently after midnight; the hour
when the family come home; Sunday-
evening tea before the fire! I have never
missed one moment of beauty, not ever
taken it for granted.

—Agnes Turnbull

Surprises

Into all our lives, in many simple, familiar, homely ways, God infuses this element of joy from the surprises of life, which unexpectedly brighten our days, and fill our eyes with light. He drops this added sweetness into His children's cup, and makes it to run over. The success we are not counting on, the blessing we were not trying after, the strain of music in the midst of drudgery, the beautiful morning picture or sunset glory thrown in as we pass to or from our daily business, the unsought word of encouragement or expression of sympathy, the sentence that meant for us more than a writer or speaker thought— these and a hundred others that everyone's experience can supply are instances of what I mean.

—*Samuel Longfellow*

The Day

The day will bring some lovely thing,
I say it over each new dawn;
"Some gay, adventurous thing to hold
Against my heart, when it is gone."
And so I rise and go to meet
The day with wings upon my feet.

I come upon it unaware—
Some sudden beauty without name;
A snatch of song, a breath of pine;
A poem lit with golden flame;
High tangled bird notes, keenly thinned,
Like flying color on the wing.

No day has ever failed me quite—
Before the grayest day is done,
I come upon some misty bloom
Or a late line of crimson sun.
Each night I pause, remembering
Some gay, adventurous, lovely thing.

—*Grace Noll Crowell*

 THE BEST IS YET TO BE

Grow old along with me!
The best is yet to be,
The last of life, for which
    the first was made:
Our times are in His hand
Who saith "A whole I planned,
Youth shows but half; trust God:
    see all nor be afraid!"

— Robert Browning

I shall grow old,
    but never lose life's zest,
Because the road's last turn
    will be the best.

—Henry van Dyke

The Best Part

Though I am growing old, I maintain that the best part is yet to come—the time when one may see things more dispassionately and know oneself and others more truly, and perhaps be able to do more, and in religion rest centered in a few simple truths. I do not want to ignore the other side, that one will not be able to see so well or walk so far or read so much. But there may be more peace within more communion with God, more real light instead of distraction about many things, better relations with others, fewer mistakes.

—*Benjamin Jowett*

That we are bound to the earth does not mean that we cannot grow . . .

—C. G. Jung

We are put here to grow, and we ought to grow, and to use all the means of growth according to the laws of our being. The only real satisfaction there is, is to be growing up inwardly all the time . . .

—James Freeman Clarke

I find the great thing in this world is not so much where we stand, as in what direction we are moving.

— Oliver Wendell Holmes

To be what we are, and to become what we are capable of becoming, is the only end of life.

—Robert Louis Stevenson

Whatever you can do, or dream you can,
Begin it.

—*Johann Wolfgang von Goethe*

Keep true to the dreams of thy youth.

—*Johann von Schiller*

To fulfil the dreams of one's youth; that is
the best that can happen to a man. No
worldly success can take the place of that.

—*Willa Cather*

The dreams of childhood . . . so good to be
believed in once, so good to be remem-
bered when outgrown.

—*Charles Dickens*

Into my heart's treasury
I slipped a coin
That time cannot take
Nor a thief purloin—
Oh better than the minting
Of a gold-crowned king
Is the safe-kept memory
Of a lovely thing.

—Sara Teasdale

God has given us memory that we might
have roses in December.

—James M. Barrie

The great thing about getting older is that
you don't lose all of the other ages
you've been.

—*Madeleine L'Engle*

So life's year begins and closes;
Days though shortening still can shine . . .

—*Thomas Moore*

Flowers are lovely; love is flower-like;
Friendship is a sheltering tree;—
Oh the joys that came down shower-like,
Of friendship, love, and liberty,
Ere I was old!

—*Samuel Taylor Coleridge*

Birthday

At first I said: "I will not have, I think,
A cake this year. I'm much too old for it."
And then, "Perhaps a cake
   but, oh! no pink
Candles for folks to count
   when they are lit."
Then I said later, "Well, perhaps, a few
Small candles *would* make
   the affair more bright;
But the true number—it would never do!"
And yet today when I stood up to light
A candle-flame for each year
   I have come,
I laughed, and how my spirit
   sang in me!
I was most proud (although my hands
   shook some)
As I held up the cake for all to see—
Years I have worked in, played in,
   and been sad,
Years I have loved in, lived in,
   and been glad!

                 —Elaine V. Emans

Time

As you grow older, more than ever before you need to spend part of each day alone in peace, quiet, and meditation; and in prayer that you may be shown how to continue to live each day with courage, kindness, wisdom, laughter, interest, and understanding. You should take time to absorb and enjoy the lovely world in which you live and come to know its inhabitants with affectionate amusement.

—*William B. Terhune*

Let Me Grow Lovely

Let me grow lovely, growing old—
So many fine things do:
Laces, and ivory, and gold,
And silks need not be new;
And there is healing in old trees,
Old streets a glamour hold;
Why may not I, as well as these,
Grow lovely, growing old?

—*Karle Wilson Baker*

As I Grow Old

God keep my heart
   attuned to laughter
When youth is done;
When all the days are
   gray days, coming after
The warmth, the sun.
God keep me then from
   bitterness, from grieving,
When life seems cold;
God keep me always
   loving and believing
As I grow old.

                      —Author Unknown

How Old Are You?

Age is a quality of mind.
If you have left your dreams behind,
If hope is cold,
If you no longer look ahead,
If your ambitions' fires are dead—
Then you are old.

But if from life you take the best,
And if in life you keep the jest,
If love you hold;
No matter how the years go by,
No matter how the birthdays fly—
You are not old.

—H. S. Fritsch

Youth is not a time of life; it is a state of mind . . .

—*Samuel Ullman*

So long as enthusiasm lasts, so long is youth still with us.

—*David S. Jordan*

We must always have old memories and young hopes.

—*Arsène Houssaye*